D1558663

The Kabbalistic Bible

by Rabbi Tanhuma

© Copyright 2006 – BN Publishing

ISBN   9562913260

www.bnpublishing.com

info@bnpublishing.com

Printed in the U.S.A.

The

Kabbalistic

Bible

The Kabbalistic Bible

The Torah is full of holy fire; it was written with a black fire upon a white fire.

The Torah has meekness as its footgear, and the fear of God as its crown. Hence Moses was the proper person through whose hands it should be delivered; he was meek, and with the fear of the Lord he was crowned.

You can not expect to occupy yourself with the study of the Torah in the future world and receive the reward for so doing in this world; you are meant to make the Torah your own in this life, and to look for reward in the life to come.

Cain's offering consisted of the seed of flax, and that of Abel of the fatlings of his sheep. This is probably the reason why the wearing of a garment of various materials, as of woolen and linen together, was prohibited.

As one who finishes the building of his house proclaims that day a holiday, and consecrates the building, so God, having finished creation in the six days, proclaimed the seventh day a holy day and sanctified it.

If the fraudulent man and the usurer offer to make restitution, it is not permitted to accept it from them.

The Bible, or written law, contains unexplained passages and hidden sentences, which can not be fully understood without the help of the oral law. Further, the written law contains generalities, whilst the oral law goes in for explanations in detail, and is consequently much larger in volume.

Indeed, as a figure of speech we could apply to it the words in Job (iv. 9),

"The measure thereof is longer than the earth and broader than the sea."

The knowledge of this oral law can not be expected to be found amongst those who are bent on enjoying earthly life and worldly pleasures; its acquisition requires the relinquishment of all worldliness, riches and pleasures, and requires intellect aided by constant study.

There is no evil that has no remedy, and the remedy for sin is repentance.

Whatever hardships may be imposed upon Jews by the powers that be, they must not rebel against the authorities who impose them, but are to render compliance, except when ordered to disregard the Torah and its injunctions; for that would be tantamount to giving up their God.

He that stole an ox had to restore fivefold, and he that stole a sheep had to give back only fourfold, because by stealing the ox he may have prevented the owner from plowing or doing other agricultural work for the time being.

There is a wall of separation erected between the Shechinah and the following three classes, a wall that can never be razed: The cheat, the robber, and the idle worshiper.

The meaning of the phrase, "God made man in his own image," is that, like his Maker, a man is to be righteous and upright. Do not argue that evil inclination is innate in you; such argument is fallacious; when you are a child you commit no sin; it is when you grow out of infancy that your evil inclination becomes developed. You have the power of resisting the evil inclination if you feel so inclined, even as you are able to convert the bitter elements of certain foods into very palatable eatables.

Hadrian King of Rome (Edom), having made great conquests, requested his court in Rome to proclaim him God. In answer to this modest request, one of his ministers said, "If your Majesty desires to become God, it will be necessary to quit God's property first, to show your independence of him. He created heaven and earth; get out of these and you can proclaim yourself God." Another counselor replied by asking Hadrian to help him out of a sad position in which he was placed. "I have sent a ship to sea," he said, "with all my possessions on board of her, and she is but a short distance - about three miles from shore - but is struggling against the watery elements, which threaten her total destruction." "Do not trouble," replied the King, "I will send some of my ships well manned, and your craft shall be brought to the haven where she would be." "There is no need for all that," said the counselor satirically; "order but a little favorable wind, and her own crew will manage to bring her safely into port." "And where shall I order the wind from? How have I the power to order the wind?"answered Hadrian angrily. Has your Majesty not even a little wind at your command?" said the King's adviser mockingly, "and yet you wish to be proclaimed God!"

Hadrian then retired to his own rooms angry and disappointed, and when he told his wife of the controversy he had had with his ministers she remarked that his advisers did not strike on the proper thing which would bring his wish to a happy consummation. "It seems to me," she said mockingly, "that the first thing you must do is to give God back what he has given you and be under no obligation to him." "And what may that be?" inquired the heathen.

"The soul, of course," answered his wife. "But," argued the King, "if I give back my soul, I shall not live." "Then," said his wife triumphantly, "that shows that you are but mortal, and can not be God."

The slanderer seems to deny the existence of God. As King David has it, "They say, Our lips are with us, who is Lord over us?" (Ps. xii.)

Let us not lose sight of the lesson that it is meant to convey to us by the expression, "And the Lord came down to see" (Gen. xi.), namely that we are not to judge merely by "hearsay" and to assert anything as having taken place unless we saw it.

Elijah quickened the dead, caused rain to descend, prevented rain from coming down, and brought fire down from heaven; but he did not say " I am God."

When Noah set out to plant the vine, Satan encountered him and asked upon what errand he was bent" I am going to plant the vine," said Noah. "I will gladly assist you in this good work," said Satan. When the offer of help was accepted Satan brought a sheep and slaughtered it on the plant, then a lion, then a pig, and finally a monkey. He thus explained these symbols to Noah. When a man tastes the first few drops of wine he will be as harmless as a sheep; when he tastes a little more he will become possessed of the courage of a lion and think himself as strong; should he further indulge in the liquid produced by your plant he will become as objectionable as a pig; and by yet further indulgence in it he will become like a monkey.

Because the Torah mulcts the thief in double, and in some cases more than double, the value of what he has stolen, one is not to conclude that he is allowed to steal when in want, with the intention of paying back double and more than double the value.

The promise to Abraham that he should become a great nation was fulfilled when the Israelites became the recipients of God's laws. Moses, on account of their being the possessors of the Torah, styles them "a great nation " (Deut. iv.).

Blessings proceed from Zion (Ps. cxxxiv.), the dew is blessed from Zion (Ps. cxxxiii.), so does help come from Zion (Ps. xx.), and salvation (Ps. xiv.). The future blessings of Israel will proceed from Zion (Ps. cxiii.), and Zion itself will receive God's blessings.

The comparison in beauty of any woman to Sarah is like comparing monkeys with men.

"This shall not be thine heir, but he that cometh forth out of thy loins shall be thine heir" (Gen. xv. 4). There is a story of a man blessed with learning, wisdom, and riches, who had an only son, to whom be naturally gave the best education, and whom he sent to Jerusalem for the purpose of completing his education. He bad all arrangements made for his bodily comforts, and took every care that the young man, who was very promising and on whom he doted, should want for nothing. Shortly after his son's departure, he took to his bed, from which he rose not again.

His death caused immense regret in the place of his residence, for in him the poor had lost a real support, and many a man a wise counselor and adviser. It was felt that the town in general had lost one whom it would be difficult to replace.

The funeral and the days of mourning over, a friend who was known to be the executor of the dead man's last will, and who had duly informed the son by letter of the sad death of his father, proceeded to break the seal of the will and see its contents. To his great astonishment, and no less to the astonishment of every one who learned the nature of its contents, the whole of the dead man's property, personal and otherwise, movable and immovable, after leaving considerable amounts to various charities, was left to his negro slave; there was but a saving clause that his beloved son should have the privilege of choosing one thing, but one only, out of the whole estate.

The son, though duly informed of the details of this strange will, was so immersed in grief at the Ion of his father that his mind could not be diverted to anything else; and it was only when his teacher alluded to his father's death and the inheritance which he might expect, and advised him to use it for the same laudable purposes, that the young man informed his beloved master that by his father's will he had been reduced to a beggar. Meanwhile, the negro slave of the departed man, having gone through all the formalities and proved his title, lost no time in taking possession of his dead master's property. He was ready and willing enough to grant the son one thing out of his late father's goods, whenever he should come and claim the object of his choice. The acute rabbi, on reading the will, saw at once the drift of the testator's intention, and told his pupil that he should proceed to his native town and take possession of his property. "But I have no property to take possession of," pleaded the young man, "except one article of my late father's goods." "Well then," replied the teacher, unable to conceal a smile, "choose your late father's negro slave out of his estate, and with him will go over to you all he possesses, since a slave can own nothing, and all he has belongs to his master. That, indeed, was your father's clever device. He knew that if the will were to state that all was left to you, the negro, being by the force of circumstances in charge of everything that was left, would probably in your absence take for himself and his friends all the valuables on which be could lay his hands; whereas if he knew or thought an belonged to him he would take care of everything that was left. Your wise father knew that the one thing he gave you the power to choose would be no other than his slave, and with him you would become the just and rightful owner of everything."

You can not be too careful about prayer, and you should never omit to pray. Prayer eclipses all other services, and towers above sacrifices; and the sinful man may receive God's grace through prayer.

As one is prohibited from reciting any portion of the Torah by heart, but must read it out of the written scroll, so is he who expounds any portion thereof not allowed to read his exposition from anything written, but must deliver it by word of mouth.

When God's creatures incur punishment, the Merciful One looks for one to plead for the guilty people, to open a way, as it were, as was the case in the time of Jeremiah. (See Jer. v.)

The proverb says, "If you rub shoulders with the anointed you will become anointed."Lot, being associated with Abraham, became hospitable; whilst his character does not indicate inclination to hospitality on his own part.

You must not in any way mislead your fellow men, not even to the extent of asking the price of anything he may have for disposal, so ag to make him believe that you are a likely purchaser, whilst you have no intention of purchasing the article.

The righteous are put to more and severer trials than the unrighteous. So the owner of flax will beat out the good flax often and severely, so as to make it purer, but does not treat the inferior article in the same way, lest it fall away into small pieces.

The following tend to make a man prematurely old: Fear, war, trouble from his children, or a shrew of a wife.

As there is a regularity in the position of the sun daily three times: in the morning he is in the east, at noon between the east and west, and in the evening in the west, so must there be an inflexible regularity with every Jew in reciting his Prayers three times daily, morning, afternoon, and evening.

A widower with unmarried sons is advised to see his sons married before he marries again.

Adrianus (Hadrian), discussing with Rabbi Joshua the innumerable adversaries that the Israelites had to encounter, said, "Great is the sheep that can withstand seventy wolves." Rabbi Joshua replied, "Greatest is the shepherd who enables the sheep to outlive the constant attacks of the wolves."

There is merit and even dignity in handicraft.

Do not say, I need not work for my living, but cast my hope on God who supports all living creatures. You must work for a livelihood, and look up to God to bless the work of your hands. Jacob, in alluding to the delivery from Laban's house, says, "God hath seen the labor of my hands" (Gen. xxxi.).

A homely domesticated wife is like the altar in the temple; and she is even an atonement as the altar was.

Isaiah committed sin by saying, "In the midst of a people of unclean lips do I dwell" (Isa. vi.). For this, the slander which is compared to fire, he was punished with fire, with the live coal taken from the altar (Isa. vi.).

However adverse one's opinion may be of any one placed in a high position, he is bound to pay him the respect due to his position. Rabbi Judah Hannasi, when writing to Antoninus, invariably used the phrase, "Judah, thy servant, sends greeting."

A modest woman is worthy of being the wife of a high priest, for she is like an altar in her home.

God wishes man to ask forgiveness, and not to see him in his guilt.

So exceedingly handsome was Joseph that when the friends Of Potiphar's wife visited her, and the hostess proffered them fruit, the Egyptian women cut their fingers instead of the fruit, as they could not take their eyes off the wonderfully handsome Hebrew slave; and they sympathized with their friend when he scorned her advances.

Give me the admonition of the old in preference to the flattery of the young.

When Moses said to the people, "After the Lord your God shall ye walk" (Deut. xiii.), they took alarm at the formidable, or rather impossible, task imposed upon them. "How," said they, "is it possible for man to walk after God, who hath his way in the storm and in the whirlwind, and the clouds are the dust of his feet" (Nahum i.), "whose way is in the sea and his path in the great waters "? (Ps. lxxvii.). Moses explained to them that to walk after God meant to imitate humbly his attributes of mercy and compassion by clothing the naked, visiting the sick, and comforting the mourner.

A fatality seems to have been attached to Shechem. in connection with Israel's sorrows. The capture of Dinah took place at Shechem. Joseph was sold there into slavery. David's kingdom was split in Shechem; and thd advent of Jeroboam also took place in Shechem.

O woman, what mischief thou causest! Even the worshiping of idols did not cause such trouble and loss of life as a woman caused. The making and worshiping of the golden calf caused the loss of three thousand men (Exod. xxxii.) ; but through a woman at Shittim twenty-four thousand were the victims.

Good men lift up their eyes and look one straight in the face; bad, wicked men drop their eyes.

"Should not a man pray every hour?" asked Antoninus of his friend Rabbi Judah Hannasi. He demurred on receiving a reply in the negative. After a while the Rabbi called on Antoninus, and was as careful as always to address him with considerable deference.

After about an hour he came again, and addressed him again carefully with all the titles he was wont to use, and so the Rabbi repeated his visits and expressions of homage about every hour during the day. When, at last Antoninus told his friend that he felt himself slighted instead of honored by the frequency of the visits, and the expressions of homage with which Rabbi Judah meant to honor him, "Therein," the sage said, "lies my reason for telling you that man was not to address the throne of mercy every hour as you contended, since such frequency savors of contempt."

There is a most remarkable identity between the occurrences in the life of Joseph and those in the history of Zion and Jerusalem, and a remarkable similarity in the phrases employed in describing the respective events of each, whether in their adversity or in their prosperity. We read: "Israel loved Joseph" (Gen. xxxvii.), "The Lord loveth the gates of Zion" (Ps. lxxxvii.). Joseph's brethren hated him; "My heritage is unto me as a lion in the forest, it crieth out against me, therefore I hate it " (Jer. xii.). Joseph speaks of making sheaves; there are sheaves in connection with Zion (Ps. cxxvi.). Joseph dreamed: "When the Lord turned again the captivity of Zion we were like them that dream" (Ps. cxxvi.). Joseph was asked, "Wilt thou rule over us?" "Say unto Zion thy God ruleth" (Isa. Iii.). Joseph was asked whether his father and brothers would prostrate themselves before him. "They shall bow down to thee with their face toward the earth" (Isa. xlix.). Joseph's brethren were jealous; "Thus said the Lord of Hosts, I was jealous for Zion with great jealousy " (Zech. viii.). Joseph went to inquire about the peace of his brothers; Zion was to seek the peace of the city where she is captive (Jer. xxix.). - Joseph's brethren saw him from the distance; the same is said about Zion (Ezek. xxiii.). Joseph's brothers contemplated his destruction; so the nations contemplated the destruction of Zion (Ps. lxxxiii.). Joseph was stripped of his coat of many colors; concerning Zion, the prophet says, " They shall strip thee of thy clothes" (Ezek. xvi.). Joseph was put into a pit; "They have put me alive into the dungeon" (lam. iii.). The pit into which Joseph was put contained no water. In connection with Zion, Jeremiah was put into a pit where there was no water (Jer. xxxviii.). Joseph's brothers sat down to their meal; "We have given the hand to Egyptians and to Assyrians to be satisfied with bread" (Lam. v.). Joseph was pulled up from the pit; Jeremiah, who in connection with his prophecy about Zion was put into a dungeon -as stated above - was drawn up from the dungeon (Jer.

iii.). Lamentations were raised about Joseph; " And in that day did the Lord call for weeping and mourning" (Isa. xxii.). In the case of Joseph consolation was rejected. " Labor not to comfort me" (Isa. xxii.) - Joseph was sold; " the children of Judah and of Jerusalem have you sold unto the Grecians " (Joel iv.). Joseph is described as handsome; " Beautiful for situation, the joy of the whole earth, is mount Zion " (Ps. xlviii.). Joseph was the greatest in his master's house; " the glory of the latter house shall be greater than the former" (Hag. ii.). The Lord was with Joseph; "Now mine eyes shall be open and mine ears attent unto the prayers that are made in this place" (2 Chron. vii.). Grace and loving kindness were shown to Joseph; concerning Zion God says, " I remember the kindness of thy youth, the love of thine espousals " (Jer. ii.). Joseph was rendered presentable by changing his clothes, etc.; "When the Lord shall have washed away the filth of the daughters of Zion " (Isa. iv.). The throne of Pharaoh was above Joseph; " At that time they shall call Jerusalem the throne of the Lord " (Jer. iii.). Joseph was clothed, in grand garments; "Awake, awake, put on thy strength, O Zion, put on thy beautiful garments " (Isa. lii.). Joseph was met by an angel; " Behold I will send my messenger, and he shall prepare the way " (Mal. iii.).

There is a tendency with every man to become humble when near his death.

It matters not where the body is buried; the spirit goes whither it is destined.

Jacob's objection to being buried in Egypt was due to the fact that the Egyptians practised witchcraft by means of dead bodies, and be would not have his body utilized for such abominable practises.

There is no death to the righteous.

The righteous bless their offspring before they depart hence.

David was descended from Judah.

"Behold how good and how pleasant it is for brethren to dwell together "- or in unity (Ps. cxxxiii.). "O that thou wert as my brother" (Songs viii.). There are brothers and brothers. Cain and Abel were brothers, but the former slew the latter. Ishmael and Isaac were brothers, but there was no love lost between them. Jacob and Esau had no brotherly love for one another, nor did Joseph and his brothers show much love between them. David and Solomon had in their minds Moses and Aaron as typical brothers. One of the reasons why Moses so persistently hesitated to be the messenger to Pharaoh was his consideration for his brother Aaron, who was older and more eloquent than he, so that be hesitated to usurp what he considered should be Aaron's function. God, who knows the innermost thoughts of man, knew the real motive of Moses's refusal to accept the mission. Therefore we find God telling Moses, " Behold Aaron the Levite, thy brother, I know that he can speak well, and also behold be cometh forth to meet thee, and when he seeth thee he will be glad in his heart " (Exod. iv.). And as Aaron's delight at his younger brother's elevation was so great - for the phrade " glad in his heart " conveys his great delight - he was rewarded in that the Urim. and Thummim were on his heart (Exod. xxviii.). When Aaron met his brother in the mount of God he kissed him (Exod. iv.).

The staff of Moses had the initials of the names of the ten plagues written on it, in order that Moses should know in which order they were consecutively to be brought on Pharaoh and the Egyptians.

When we are told that Pharaoh took six hundred chosen chariots with which to pursue the Israelites, we are naturally met with the question whence he got those six hundred chosen chariots. He could not have obtained them from his people the Egyptians, for we find that " all the cattle of the Egyptians died " (Exod. ix.). They could not have been his own, for his own cattle also perished (Exod. ix.). Nor did the Israelites supply them, since they left with an their cattle; there was not a hoof to be left.

The explanation is found in the fact that those who feared the word of the Lord among the servants of Pharaoh made their cattle flee into the house when the bail was predicted (Exod. ix.), and these "fearers of the word of the Lord" among the Egyptians supplied Pharaoh with their animals for the purpose of pursuing the Israelites. By the character of those among the Egyptians who " feared the word of the Lord " that of the nation can be judged.

" Fear not, thou worm Jacob," says the prophet (Isa. xli.). Why was Israel compared to a worm? As the insignificant worm is able to destroy a big cedar with no other weapon than its small weak mouth, even so is Israel able to prevail against his great persecutors with no other weapon but the prayers emanating from troubled hearts and uttered with the mouth.

How great is faith! It secures happiness and salvation. Abraham's faith was accounted to him as righteousness. It was the faith which the Israelites had that redeemed them from Egypt (Exod. iv. 31). Their faith on the bank of the Red Sea carried them over that sea and brought them to the land of promise. The Lord keepeth the faithful (Pa. xxxi.). The righteous liveth by his faith (Habak. ii.). The last redemption of Israel will only be effected through faith. See bow King David values faith (Pa. cv.). Concerning faith, David says, "This is the gate of the Lord, the righteous shall enter therein."

The lifting up of Moses's hands did not defeat Amalek, nor did the copper serpent stay the biting of the burning serpents. It was the directing by these of the hearts of the Israelites, with their prayers heavenward, that defeated Amalek and caused the fiery serpents to cease.

If you have acquired knowledge, do not simultaneously acquire a haughty spirit on account of your knowledge; and if you intend to expound God's word, recite to yourself twice or thrice what you intend saying. Even so great a man as Rabbi Akiba, whenonce called upon in the assembly to get up and preach, declined to do so, on the ground that he never preached unless he rehearsed his intended speech twice or thrice to himself.

Whilst man is not to seek public notoriety and distinction, he is not to err on the side of modesty and seclusion, and refuse to give his services in communal matters.

Rabbi Asy, when approaching death, was visited by his nephew, who found the patient very depressed. "Death," said his nephew, "should not in your ease be attended with feelings of alarm. Think what you leave behind you, the learning you have acquired and imparted to an army of students, the charity you have practised, and the kindly acts you have done; is there any good that it was in your power to do that you have left undone? And you have been so modest withal; you have always eschewed putting yourself forward or seeking notoriety, and have not mixed in disputes and in communal matters."

" This," replied the good man, " even if all the good you said about me were quite correct, this alone would be sufficient cause for my depression, for I might perhaps have been able to render some service, had I not kept to myself but taken upon me the burden of communal affairs."

With idol-worshipers it is the habit to treat their gods according to the circumstances in which they find themselves, which they attribute -to' the actions of their gods. If their condition is favorable, they pay tribute to their god. " Therefore they sacrifice unto their net, and burn incense unto their drag, because by them their portion is fat and their meat plenteous," says the prophet (Habak. i.). If, on the other hand, adversities overtake them, they vent their anger on their gods.

"And it shall come to pass," the prophet tells us, " that when they shall be hungry they shall fret themselves and curse their king and their god (Isa. viii.). Not so shall you do, my people, whose destiny is shaped out by the Creator of heaven and earth. Whatever befalls you, give thanks and praise unto your God. Are you in prosperity? do not forget the Giver; do not say in your heart, " My power and the might of mine hand hath gotten me this wealth," but like David say, " I will lift up the cup of salvation and call upon the name of my God." If adversity overtakes you, if sorrow and trouble overtake you in the midst of the smooth current of your affairs, take up David's words again and say, " I found trouble and sorrow, then I called upon the name of my God."

The altar of God was to prolong man's life, and iron is a metal which can destroy man's life; therefore it was forbidden to use iron in the erection of the altar.

Slight no man. Every man was created in God's image.

Onkeles, the nephew of Hadrian - his sister's son - being anxious to embrace Judaism, yet being afraid of his uncle, told him that he wished to embark on a certain enterprise. When Hadrian offered him some money he refused to accept it, but said he wanted his uncle's advice, as he was inexperienced in the ways of the world. "Purchase goods," replied his uncle, "which do not, at present, command a high price, and are not favorites in the market, but for which there is reason to believe a demand at higher prices will eventually arise." Onkeles betook himself to Palestine, and gave himself up to study. After a time Rabbi Eliezer and Rabbi Joshua recognized in him the face of a student; they took him in hand, solved all the difficult problems he put before them, and generally befriended him. On his return home he again visited his uncle Hadrian, who, noticing that his nephew did not look as well as was his wont, inquired whether he had met with any monetary reverses in his new enterprise, or had been injured in any way. "I have met with no monetary losses," said Onkeles, " and as your nephew I am not likely to be hurt by any one." Being further pressed for the reason of his poor looks, Onkeles told his uncle they were due to his excessive studies and to the fact that he bad undergone circumcision. "And who told you to do such a thing as to undergo circumcision? " demanded Hadrian. "I acted on your advice," replied Onkeles. "I have acquired a thing that stands at a low price just now, but will eventually rise in value. I found no nation in such low esteem and so sure to rise in value as Israel. For thus said the Lord, We Redeemer of Israel and his Holy One, to him whom man despiseth, to him whom the nation abhorreth, to a servant of rulers, kings shall see and arise and princes also shall worship, because of the Lord that is faithful and the Holy One of

Israel, he shall choose them 11 (Isa. xlix.). One of Hadrian's counselors advised his master to visit his nephew's misdeed with death, for which advice the adviser received such a sharp rebuke from Hadrian that he committed suicide. Hadrian, after the death of his minister, further discussed with his nephew the matter of his conversion, and again asked for the reason of circumcision. Onkeles, asked his uncle whether he had ever bestowed any distinction on any of his army who were not willing and ready to fight for his Majesty and for the country at the risk of life. " Neither could I be received into the fold of those to whom God has given his behests and statutes without having the seal of those great statutes put on me even at the risk of my life."

Whilst the Torah teaches peace and good-will to ones fellow man, it likewise teaches the necessity of standing up against evil deeds and even rebuking the evil-doer. Moreover, though all reverence and deference are due to one's teacher, yet in the matter of censurable conduct it becomes the pupil's duty to protest against it. Bad conduct is contaminating. One is apt to fall into the same error if one sees any evil act and does not lift up one's voice to protest against it.

He who rebukes his fellow man with a sincere desire to make him better comes within the inner walls of the heavenly pavilion.

You are not permitted to select injunctions of the Torah which you consent to observe, and reject others for the observance of which you can find no reason. In accepting God's word one is bound to implicit obedience to it, the rich should ever bear in mind that his wealth may merely have been deposited with him to be a steward over it, or to test what use he will make of his possessions. Not less should the poor remember that his trials may have been sent as a test of his fortitude.

Poverty outweighs all other sorrows.

"If you have taken a pledge from the poor," says God to the rich, "do not say he is your debtor and you are therefore justified in retaining his garment. Remember you are my debtor, your life is in my hand. I return you all your senses and all your faculties after your sleep every day."

Jewish litigants are to bring their disputes for adjustment before a Jewish court, and not to have recourse to outside tribunals.

Although witnesses have always to give their evidence standing, yet an exception may be made in the case of a distinguished (learned) man, who may be allowed to sit whilst giving evidence. Should he consider it beneath his dignity to give evidence at all, be may be exempted. This only applies to any suit regarding money matters (civil cases), but in criminal matters he is not to be exempted.

God's works accommodate one another without asking any interest. The day accommodates the night, and the night the day (according to season). The moon borrows from the stars, and the stars from the moon. The higher wisdom borrows from the simple or common sense; kindness borrows from charity, the heavens from the earth, and the earth from the heavens. The Torah borrows from righteousness, and righteousness from the Torah; all without charging any interest. Is man, and man only, not to extend a helping hand to his fellow man without exacting usury for a kind act?

Regarding the giving of alms, judgment and discretion should be exercised. Obviously, poor relatives have a prior claim to any other, and the poor of your town claim priority over those of another town.

" He who hath pity on the poor lendeth unto the Lord," says Solomon (Prov. xim). It is surely good enough for you, O man, to be God's creditor. Not that he will return to you exactly the coin you give to the poor; he will look even further into your deed. The poor man was perhaps famishing, and your timely help may have rescuea him from an untimely death; God, whose creditor you have become when you helped the helpless, will rescue you and yours from danger when it is near.

He who by usury and ill-gotten gain increaseth his substance, it sball be taken from him by him who pities the poor (Prov. xxviii.). When a non-Jew wants to borrow of you, you will perhaps say that since you are not permitted to take usury from your own compatriot you may take it from a nonJew. Be assured that such ill-gotten gain will be taken from you; probably by the authorities, to erect baths or other sanitary buildings for the poor or the stranger.

Why, asked Turnus Rufus, a heathen King, of Rabbi Akiba, have we incurred the hatred of your God so that He says, "I hate Esau "? (Mal. iii.). The Rabbi said he would reply to the question the next day. On his making his appearance the following day, the King, thinking that Rabbi Akiba bad postponed the answer the day before in order to invent meanwhile some lame explanation, said to the sage satirically, " Well, Akiba, what have you dreamt during the night?" Rabbi Akiba, taking the very question as the text for his reply, said, "I dreamed I became possessed of two dogs which I named Rufus and Rufina" (the names of the questioner and his wife).

The King, in a great fury, asked Rabbi Akiba how he dared offer him and his queen so gross an insult as to name his dogs by their names. " Wherefore this indignation?" returned R. Akiba calmly; "you and yours are God's creatures, so are dogs God's creatures; you eat and drink, produce your species, live, decay, and die; all this is also the case with dogs. Yet what umbrage you take because they bear the same name as you! Consider then that God stretched forth the heavens and laid the foundations of the Earth, is the Creator, Governor, and Ruler of all animate and inanimate things; yet you make an idol of wood and stone, worship it and call it by the name of God. Should you not then incur his hatred?"

A distinguished scholar was on a voyage at sea, and on board the same ship were some merchants with their goods. In the course of conversation they asked the scholar what was the nature of his goods. "My goods," he replied, " are invaluable." Knowing, however, that there was no cargo of his on board the ship, they ridiculed his assertion. After sailing some distance from shore the ship was overtaken by pirates, who robbed the ship of its cargo and took the very clothes the passengers were wearing, so far as they were of any value. Passengers and crew were only too thankful to escape with their lives and to clothe themselves with the rags which the pirates rejected. The scholar, as he did not wear any valuable clothes, was spared by the pirates as not being worth robbing, and landed at a small town, together with his fellow passengers, who made a sorry sight in the rags that served them as clothes. The learned man, whose reputation had gone before him, was asked and consented to deliver lectures on various scientific subjects, which he handled in a masterly fashion. The lectures excited great interest, and attracted large audiences from all the neighboring towns, with the result that the man not only found his lectures remunerative from a pecuniary point of view, but soon won the friendship of the leading men of the place, where he settled down and became an influential member of the community. Fate did not smile quite so kindly on his former fellow passengers, who, having unfortunately lost all their possessions, having no trade or profession, and being clothed in rags, found it impossible to get employment. Seeing the great position the professor held in the town, they called upon him and solicited the favor of his influence on their behalf.

This he unhesitatingly and ungrudgingly gave them; he procured employment for them, and reminded them how perfectly justified he was in styling his goods invaluable.

On several occasions the Israelites were numbered, a census taken. Nor as the owner of a flock of sheep is anxious to know how many he possesses, when anything untoward happens, when a wolf has been in their midst, he is again anxious to ascertain what loss has been sustained by the mishap. Thus Moses had

the people numbered to see what loss there was after their punishment for making the golden calf.

Poor ignorant man, you want to find out God's ways; explain first the phenomenon of your own eye; it consists of white and black, and according to all reason the white should supply light, but in reality the little spot in the center of your eye is the lens to give you sight.

A man however so learned should not preach if his preaching is not agreeable to his audience.

A public teacher (preacher) must not only be thoroughly conversant with the twenty-four books of the Bible, but must be known to his flock as modest and distinguished for hiq virtues.

Moses, in spite of his being the mediator between God and his people in promulgating God's behests to them, and knowing God's intention of giving his law to his people Israel, in spite of all his varied and most wonderful qualities, and his having been in the mountain forty days and forty nights, during which he ate no bread and drank no water, in spite of all this, he is only looked upon as an earthly, a mortal being, the greatest of men, but only a mortal man.

There were forty thousand of the mixed multitude, who forced themselves on the Israelites at the Exodus and came out with them from Egypt. Among them were the two great Egyptian magicians of Pharaoh who imitated Moses's miracles before Pharaoh. Their names were Junus and Jumburius.

The living always have to arrange for the dead, such as bringing them to their resting-place, etc., but the dead are not called upon to provide anything for the living; yet behold, when any serious trouble or threats overtook the Israelites, though there were many righteous men in the camp, Moses, in his intercession had no recourse to them, but fell back upon those who had long since departed. " Remember," he prayed, " thy servants Abraham, Isaac, and Jacob." Solomon alluded to this when be said, " Wherefore

I praised the dead which are already dead
more than the living, which are yet alive "
(Eccles. iv.).

The " Mishna. " would have been
incorporated with the written Torah, but
God saw that the Torah would eventually
be translated into Greek and published as
though it were the code entrusted to
Greeks. Had the Mishna been together
with the written law, the nations would
have claimed to be the custodians of the
whole of God's word. But the oral law,
the key to and interpreter of the written
law, being entrusted to Israelites only
(which could not have been done had it
been written) the Jews alone have the
whole of God's word with the
interpretation in full.

Wisdom is granted by God to him who already possesses knowledge, not to the ignorant. A certain matron was arguing with Rabbi Jose ben Chlafta on this point of God giving wisdom to men of understanding. This, she thought, was paradoxical, as it would be more proper if God granted wisdom to simpletons, who are more in want of it than wise men.

Rabbi Jose put a simple question to her. "If two men," he asked, "were to appear before you, one wealthy and the other poor, each asking you for a loan of money, whom would you be more inclined to trust?" "Surely the one possessed of wealth," she replied. " God in his dispensation," said Rabbi Jose, "giveth wisdom to the man of understanding, who possesses and knows the value of it, and will make profitable use of the augmentation: like a man whom you would prefer to trust with your money, knowing that he has facilities to employ profitably what you lend him; whereas the fool entrusted with wisdom would abuse the precious gift and convert it into folly, like the poor man whom you would not care to trust, lest the money should be lost through his inability to employ it profitably."

Rabbi Eliezer ben Jose stated that he saw in Rome the mercy-seat of the temple. There was a bloodstain on it. On inquiry he was told that it was a stain from the blood which the high priest sprinkled thereon on the Day of Atonement.

The Torah was given in the wilderness, and, like the wilderness, it is free and open to all comers -without formalities or introductions: all that wish to do so can enter into it.

The boards for the Mishkan were made from shittim-wood, from a tree that does not bear fruit; thereby man is taught the virtue of economy: he should not waste anything of greater value when the same can be obtained by using articles of lesser value. Even the Mishkan was not to be made out of fruit-trees, since it could be made equally as effective out of trees bearing no fruit.

It is but right and proper that one should be right in the eight of God, but it is also desirable so to act as to be just and right in the eyes of man.

Slander no one, whether thy brother or not thy brother, whether a Jew or not a Jew.

In connection with the poor man's sacrifice, that of a handful of flour, and not in connection with the rich man's sacrifices (of bulls and rams) do we find the expression "and if any soul." God looked upon the poor man's offering of a handful of flour as though he had offered his life.

The righteous stand on a higher level than angels.

Those who aim at greatness do not always get it. Moses fled from it, but it was forced upon him.

God consulted the Torah when about to create man, but the Torah was dubious about calling man into existence, for since his days would be so short and his ways so perverted be would require much forbearance. God's reply was, " By thee (Torah) I declare myself as a God merciful, long-suffering, and abundant in goodness and in truth."

"Swear not at all, not even to the truth."

Future bliss can neither be imagined, explained, nor described. We know nothing of its nature, form, greatness, or beauty, its quantity or quality. This much one should know, the phrase, "the world to come," does not imply that it is a world yet to be called into existence; it exists already, but the phrase is employed to describe the life into which those who are in the present stage of existence will be transposed when they throw off this mortal coil.

The leper, the blind, the abject poor, and those who have no progeny are as though dead.

Rabbi Judah Hannasi, arriving at a place called Semunia, was entreated by the community to select a rabbi for them. He sent them Rabbi Levi ben Sissyas, a learned and able man. Not long afterward the newly appointed Rabbi came to R. Judah Hannasi, the donor of his living, and whilst thanking him for the appointment expressed the fear that his position was not tenable. On being questioned for his reasons he answered that Scriptural passages were submitted to him for solution by his congregants which it was above his capability to solve. Among others be mentioned the passage, I will show thee that which is written, and which is true (Dan. x.). Hence they argue that there must be something written and which is -not true. Rabbi Judah Hannasi then explained: "Man," he said, "incurs retribution if he leaves matters as they are, and does nothing to avert the punishment decreed upon him. In this case what is written is true: his punishment will overtake him. But on the other hand, if he reflects and thinks over his evil ways, becomes contrite, repents and asks his merciful Father for forgiveness, and the deserved punishment is held back, in this instance what is written is not true."

By this hypothesis you are to reconcile some seemingly contradictory passages in Scripture, such as in 1 Sam. (ii. 25), where in connection with Eli's sons we have it that they harkened not unto the voice of their father because the Lord wanted to slay them. But, through the prophet, God sends us a message, " As I live, saith the Lord, I have no pleasure in the death of the wicked " (Ezek. xxxiii.). The answer is that there are sinners and sinners, those who do and those who do not repent.

Two sheep and two-tenth parts of flour were demanded as an offering, whereas of wine only the smallest possible quantity was to be offered. This was a hint that wine is always to be used sparingly, as indulgence in it leads to mischief.

The guardian angels are always near God's throne, but the accusing ones are kept at a distance.

Have no undue compassion for tyrants, and you will not become a tyrant over those who deserve compassion.

As an example of good manners and the virtue of considering the feelings of others, a story is related of a distinguished man who invited friends to his son's marriage. During the feast the bridegroom himself went to the cellar to fetch some very old and costly wine for the guests, when he was fatally bitten by a snake which was hidden under the casks. When the host learned the shocking news of his son's death he refrained from disturbing his guests' enjoyment, and when the feast was over and prayers after meat were about to be pronounced, he told the assembly that there would be burial-prayers for his son, who had met his death by the bite of a snake.

At Sinai the women received and accepted the Decalogue before the men.

Palestine is destined to be the center of the globe.

Before man had yet made his appearance on earth, the angels sanctified God's name and sang hymns before him in anticipation of man's advent. The words they used for their hymns were, "Blessed be the Lord God of Israel from everlasting to everlasting." When Adam made his appearance they asked, "Is this the human creature in anticipation of whose advent we sang hymns?" They were told that this was not the one, as he would prove to be dishonest. At Noah's birth the angels exclaimed, "This time we behold the man." "No," they were told, this one will be given to "drinking." Nor did they guess well when they suggested Abraham was the right man when be made his appearance, for his progeny was Ishmael. Again they were undeceived when they hit upon Isaac as the man for whose coming they had sung hymns, for did he not beget Esau whom God hated I At the appearance of Jacob they again ventured a guess, and this time God said to them, "You have fixed on the right man. He shall be named Israel, and his descendants shall be called by his name." Hence God said to Moses, " Tell the children of Israel that they were sanctified before they were called into existence, and must therefore remain holy, even as their God is holy." So a king when bringing his newly married bride into his palace might say to her: " You are now united to me. I am king, therefore be you henceforth queen."

"When you come into the land you shall plant all manner of trees for food" (Lev. xix.). Although you will find "the land filled with all good things," yet you are not to abstain from labor, especially agriculture; you are to occupy yourselves in these pursuits. Even the old who have no reasonable expectation of eating of the fruits of their labor shall participate in the work of cultivating the ground.

The caution which King Solomon utters, "Rob not the poor" (Prov. xxii.), would seem superfluous. Who is likely to rob a poor man who has nothing to be robbed of? But his words go further than they seem to go at first sight. They mean that if you are in the habit of apportioning some of your substance to the poor it should not enter your mind to discontinue doing so. If you are tempted to say, why should I give my substance to others, remember that by your discontinuance you are robbing the poor. He and you are mine, and I may reverse the condition of things.

Regarding the ceremony of the red heifer (Numb. xix.), Rabbi Johanan ben Zakkai explained to his pupils that its ashes could not render any unclean person clean. But as this is a statute of the Torah, we must inquire for no reason. If we refused to do anything that God commands without a definite reason, we should no longer be paying him simple obedience.

In addition, he continued, supposing one of the children of the kings servants had soiled the king's palace, the mother would naturally be fetched and asked to wash out the stain which her child had made. So the mother of the calf with which the Israelites polluted God's world is called into requisition to purify the pollution made by her offspring.

Apart from the essential qualifications for the office of high priest, he had also to be handsome, healthy, in a good financial position, a man of mature judgment, and of advanced age. When he was poor, but otherwise qualified, he was placed in a position beyond want One Pinchus, "the stone-cutter," being in every respect eminently fitted for the office of high priest except that he was poor, the priests amongst themselves contributed enough to make him actually a man of affluence.

Out of certain classes of things God has chosen one. Of days, the seventh was chosen and sanctified. Of years, too, the seventh was chosen as the Sabbatical year; and out of seven Sabbatical years one was selected as the Jubilee. Of countries, God made choice of Palestine. Of the heavens, the Aroboth was chosen for God's throne. Of nations, Israel was the choice, and of the tribes of Israel, that of Levi.

God blessed Adam, Noah, and Abraham, but he endowed Abraham with the power of blessing which the Lord will indorse.

During the twenty-six generations that passed from the creation to the giving of the Torah, the world was upheld by God's loving-kindness, which was, so to speak, the pivot upon which the world existed. When the Torah was given to and accepted by Israel, an additional support was given to the world upon which it could stand, and yet it was only like a bench standing upon two feet, not very well supported. With the erection of the Mishkan the world received a substantial support. So a stool which only stood upon two legs receives a third, and is rendered firm.

At the Exodus a compact was made with the Israelites, by which they undertook to erect the Mishkan for the Shechinah to dwell amongst them, and this is indicated in the 29th chapter of Exodus, "And they shall know that I am the Lord their God that brought them -forth out of the land of Egypt that I may dwell among them."

In order not to cause jealousy as to who should be the seventy elders, Moses cast lots by taking seventy-two slips representing six of each tribe, writing the word "elder " onseventy of the slips and leaving the two odd ones blank. Seventy-two men then drew blanks of them a slip, and those who drew blanks had to give up their claims.

The harp upon which the Levites played had seven strings.

God's behest were to be the guiding principle of the Israelite in all his doings throughout his earthly career. Plowing, sowing, reaping, threshing: these have all their laws by which he is to conduct them. In the making of dough, in killing meat, in the fruit of his trees, he has his laws, also about the hair of his head, his apparel, the building of his house, and the burying of his dead.

Orientals have some commendable habits. When they kiss they kiss the hand, not the mouth. They do not handle meat with their hands, but use knives. When they have to consider any important public matter, they assemble in the open outside the town.

The "Shekel, when mentioned in the Pentateuch, means one "sela"; in the Prophets it amounts to five and twenty "selaim"; but those in the Holy Writings (Hagiographa) are one hundred "selaim." There is an exception in the case of the "shekolim" which Ephron the Hittite asked of Abraham for the "cave of Machpelah": they also were one hundred "selaim " each.

Midian and Moab were enemies from time immemorial; but for the purpose of injuring the Israelites they overlooked their long-standing enmity: just as two dogs will very quickly desist from fighting if they see a wolf approaching, and will unite their strength against the advancing enemy. Balaam's services were so anxiously sought after because the Israelites and their leader, Moses, were known to have immense power with their mouth (prayer); therefore they wanted one who also bad great power with his eloquence.

When man confesses and says, "O God, I have sinned," the very messenger sent to punish him for that sin has his power paralyzed and his hand stayed.

To entice a man to sin is tantamount to taking his life.

If Moses had been a selfish man and had only considered himself and his own interest he would have delayed to avenge the Israelites on the Midianites as long as possible, because the duration of his earthly life was fixed for the time when he should have brought about vengeance on Midian (Numb. xxxi.). But like a faithful shepherd, unselfish and self-sacrificing as he was, he strove to consummate all his work without regarding his own life or his own interest, and as soon as that part of his duty was ripe for performance, and when it was to the advantage of his flock he set himself to do the work, knowing well that when that work was finished his earthly career was finished.

"Ye shall keep my statutes and my judgments, which if a man do he shall live in them" (Lev. xviii.): live in them, says God, but not die by them.

God gave the Torah to Israel, but all nations are to benefit by it.

Jews are under an oath not to reveal the time of redemption (those who may know it), not to prolong its consummation by their unrighteousness, and not to rebel against the ruling power.

Moses was born and died on the same day of the month, namely, the seventh day of Adar.

Moses prayed to God to show him his glory, and in compliance with that prayer God says, "I will pass all my goodness before thee" (Exod. iii.). Because God's goodness is God's glory; mercy and goodness are the brightest jewels in God's crown.

Death is designed for man from time immemorial. When the hour of man's departure hence arrives, nothing will save him from it If he had the wings of an eagle and could soar high up above the earth, he would, of his own accord, come down to meet his fate.- Death is a new gate for the righteous to enter in.

Do not weigh, as it were in scales, the importance or the insignificance of your acts, as long as they are acts of righteousness; and do not speculate and say, "I will not do is or that because it is only a small or light act in the scale of God's commandments; I will therefore rather perform a more important act, and my reward will be correspondingly greater." For this reason God hath concealed the nature of the reward for carrying out his statutes. A certain king hired workmen to cultivate his garden, but did not tell them what the reward would be for raising each kind of fruit or plant, for if he had done so the workmen would one and all have endeavored to produce the fruit for which the highest wage was promised, and the other products would have been neglected. Yet there are two commandments, one apparently of slight and the other of great importance, for which precisely the same reward is promised. (1) That of sending away the dam and retaining its young, for the carrying out of which well-being and long life are promised (Dent. xxii.); and (2) the honoring of parents, for which the same reward is assured. This tends to indorse what we maintain, that it is not for man to define the smallness or greatness of a godly act, or the nature and quality of the rewards. It is sufficient to know that the doing of God's will carries with it reward for faith and for doing it simply because we are told to do so.

Let not the Israelites be haughty and say that they only are the people who possess and live up to the commandments of God, for other nations, though not the recipients of God's laws, also have the commandments of the Lord as their life's guide, and glorify his name.

No affliction overtakes man without his having first some foreboding or warning of its coming.

No evil-doer can plead ignorance; for the two ways, the good and the evil, are so distinctly marked that it is impossible to mistake the one for the other. Moses was like the old watchman who sat on the high road where two paths, a stony and a smooth one, met, and constantly warned wayfarers which one to take.

God will eventually reveal his glory to all mankind as unmistakably as though he had placed his throne in the center of the heavens, and then moved it from one extreme end to the other, so that everybody should see and know it.

No one can imagine the reward of him who accepts all his sorrows and reverses with religious resignation.

Rabbi Akiba, in defiance of the mandate of the Grecian authorities, who prohibited the study of the Torah, was found by his friend, Prysus ben Judah, with a host of disciples, diligently pursuing his wonted research. "Knowest thou not," asked his friend, "the great danger thou art facing by thus defying the authorities? Take my advice and desist from thy studies."

"Your advice," returned Rabbi Akiba, "seems to me like the advice of the fox who., on seeing fishes swimming in a river here and there, told them to come out, and he would show them a resting-place in the rocks. 'Are you the wise one amongst the beasts of the field?' retorted the fishes. 'If in our own element we can find no rest and safety, how much worse will it be with us when we are out of it?' With us Jews the Torah is our very life (Prov. iv.). In pursuing its study I may incur the risk of losing my earthly life; in relinquishing it I face the certainty of moral and spiritual death."

The heart and mind of the priest when conducting divine service was not to be diverted by anything else; his whole heart and mind was to be concentrated upon the service.

It is not too much to say that discretion should be exercised regarding the names one gives to his children. There are instances in which a name implying evil qualities has been given to a child, and the child, when grown up into manhood, has exemplified by his life the meaning of his name.

Hope is held out here for man for everything. If he is in abject poverty, he may become rich; if he is sickly, it is not beyond the range of possibility for him to become robust; if he is captive, he may regain his liberty. Death is the only thing which man can not hope to escape. But let man take comfort in the thought that even so great a man as Moses, who spoke with God face to face, the head of all prophets, the greatest of men, did not escape death.

Notes

The Torah means the first five books of the Bible, the Law of Moses.

It is said in the Talmud that Chebore, King of Persia, laid his Jewish subjects under special tribute, and with the money thus raised he built dwellings and other accommodations for the poor. Hence the expression of the Midrash, "it will be taken from you, probably, by the authorities, to erect baths or other sanitary buildings."

BN Publishing

Improving People's Life

www.bnpublishing.com

We have Book Recommendations for you

**Automatic Wealth: The Secrets of the Millionaire Mind--
Including: Acres of Diamonds, As a Man Thinketh, I Dare
you!, The Science of Getting Rich, The Way to Wealth, and
Think and Grow Rich [UNABRIDGED]
by Napoleon Hill, et al (CD-ROM)**

**Think and Grow Rich [MP3 AUDIO] [UNABRIDGED]
by Napoleon Hill, Jason McCoy (Narrator) (Audio CD)**

**As a Man Thinketh [UNABRIDGED]
by James Allen, Jason McCoy (Narrator) (Audio CD)**

**Your Invisible Power: How to Attain Your Desires by
Letting
Your Subconscious Mind Work for You [MP3 AUDIO]
[UNABRIDGED] by Genevieve Behrend, Jason McCoy
(Narrator)
(Audio CD)**

**Thought Vibration or the Law of Attraction in the Thought
World [MP3 AUDIO] [UNABRIDGED]
by William Walker Atkinson, Jason McCoy (Narrator)
(Audio CD)**

**Thought Vibration or the Law of Attraction in the Thought
World & Your Invisible Power (Paperback)**

**The Law of Success, Volume I:
The Principles of Self-Mastery (Law of Success, Vol 1)
by Napoleon Hill (Paperback - Jun 20, 2006)**

**The Law of Success , Volume II & III:
A Definite Chief Aim & Self Confidence
by Napoleon Hill (Paperback - Aug 15, 2006)**

BN Publishing

Improving People's Life

www.bnpublishing.com

BN Publishing

Improving People's Life

www.bnpublishing.com

Breinigsville, PA USA
25 November 2009
228146BV00001B/7/A